CL

'Those w
supern
t

The Independent

'I am quite convinced she has
certain remarkable powers'
The Mail on Sunday

CLEAR
YOUR
MIND
A Little Book of Life

BETTY SHINE

HarperCollins*Publishers*

HarperCollins*Publishers*
77–85 Fulham Palace Road
Hammersmith, London W6 8JB

Published by HarperCollins*Publishers* 1998

1 3 5 7 9 8 6 4 2

Material extracted from *A Mind of Your Own*
published by HarperCollins*Publishers* 1998

Copyright © Betty Shine 1998

Betty Shine asserts the moral right to
be identified as the author of this work.

ISBN   0 00 653098 2

Printed and bound in Great Britain

Cover photographs © Telegraph Colour Library

INTRODUCTION

A Mind of Your Own was born out of the hundreds of letters I receive every day.

I was fascinated by the repetition of certain words in these letters, as these gave a clear indication of the root cause of the mental and physical problems people were experiencing.

Although this pocket version does not contain the visualisations which appear in the original text, it does not in any way detract from the healing and help you will receive. This little book will become a life-long friend and mentor. Carry it with you at all times and it will change your life.

You may find that the quotations alone carry the age-old wisdom you seek – they certainly demonstrate how we experience the same thoughts and emotions as people have for centuries. The world may change but we do not.

You will also read my own insight into each experience, and when you close the book it will still be with you in the form of an affirmation given at the end of each word.

Clear Your Mind is a little book of life. If you need more detail or visualisations, you will find them in its parent, *A Mind of Your Own*, which has already enriched the lives of many thousands of readers.

Betty Shine

ACCIDENTS

Now and then
there is a person born
who is so unlucky
that he runs into accidents
which started out to happen
to somebody else.

DON MARQUIS
1878–1937

The majority of accidents occur when people are under stress. Prevention is always better than cure – think before you act. The pace of life is getting faster, and you must steal a few moments for yourself. Not only will you live longer, but the quality of your life will be greater.

A moment's thought could save a life.

AGEING

Youth, which is forgiven everything,
forgives itself nothing:
age, which forgives itself anything,
is forgiven nothing.

GEORGE BERNARD SHAW
1856–1950

Physical ageing is inevitable, but there is a route that you can take to looking and feeling better that costs nothing. By stimulating and strengthening your mind with visualisation, you can bring about a transformation. Your body will be the same, but it will glow with health.

I feel young. I am young.

AGGRESSION

As we jog on, either laugh with me, or at me, or in short do anything – only keep your temper.

LAURENCE STERNE
1713–1768

Self-discipline is the only way to keep aggressive behaviour under control, and the best way is to explode on paper. As the thoughts come into your head, write them down, and keep writing until you have got them out of your system.

Burst the bubble and stay out of trouble.

ANGER

Anger is a short madness.

HORACE
65-8 BC

You will not often have at your disposal the amount of adrenaline that comes with anger, so use it to get some of the lousy jobs that need doing out of the way. If you have a car, wash and polish it; if the house needs cleaning, get to it. Use your imagination to get rid of that negative power surge.

The anger will not consume me.

BLESSINGS

*Look to your health; and if you have it,
praise God, and value it next to good
conscience; for health is the second blessing
that we mortals are capable of; a blessing
that money cannot buy.*

IZAAK WALTON
1593–1683

Although health is of prime importance in our lives, there are hundreds of small blessings that bring happiness into our everyday existence, and it is very comforting to remember these. Think about the small things that have made your life bearable and you will feel rejuvenated as the original pleasure that it gave you pulses through your being.

Life itself is a blessing.

CHARITY

By different methods different men excel;
But where is he who can do all things well?

CHARLES CHURCHILL
1731–1764

Charity takes little effort and can bring much pleasure. Whatever you give out will come back to you when you are at your lowest ebb, so that it will have the maximum effect.

Charity toward others will enhance my own life.

CHATTING

*You must lie upon the daisies and discourse
in novel phrases of your complicated state
of mind,
The meaning doesn't matter if it's only idle
chatter of a transcendental kind.*

W. S. GILBERT
1836–1911

What better relaxation could you find than having a chat with a friend? Hours pass as you let your hair down and bare your soul, cleansing and healing simultaneously. It will never go out of fashion and cannot be surpassed as food for the soul. Highly recommended.

Don't feel flat – have a chat.

CHEERFULNESS

I have tried too in my time to be a philosopher;
But, I don't know how, cheerfulness was always breaking in.

OLIVER EDWARDS
1711–1791

The world needs continued injections of cheerfulness. At work or at play, those who have this gift are a joy to be with and are much sought after for the light they bring into people's lives. Misery is so much easier to come by. Don't let it put out *your* light.

Spreading cheer will bring others near.

CHRISTMAS

Heap on more wood! – the wind is chill;
But let it whistle as it will,
We'll keep our Christmas merry still.

SIR WALTER SCOTT
1771–1832

Even if you are not religious, you should still perceive Christmas as a time for renewal. Looking back at the old year could give you some pointers as to how not to make the same mistakes again. Friendships can be renewed, and this is the one time in the year when love should be at the top of your list.

I will keep the spirit of Christmas throughout the year.

COMEDY

This world is a comedy to those that think,
a tragedy to those that feel.

HORACE WALPOLE,
FOURTH EARL OF ORFORD
1717–1797

If you have an ability to make people laugh, use it. It is the finest healing of all. In the home it is a talent that can prevent arguments reaching a dangerous level. At the office it can work for you if you silently perceive the funny side of difficult situations.

Laugh every day and keep misery at bay.

CONVERSATION

*Tomorrow a stranger will say with
masterly good sense precisely what we have
thought and felt all the time, and we shall
be forced to take with shame our own
opinion from another.*

RALPH WALDO EMERSON
1803–1882

Everyone has interesting thoughts but there are people who are shy and cannot open up a conversation, fearful that they might look or sound stupid. Don't worry! The art of good conversation is to open your mouth and talk. It doesn't really matter what subject you begin with, just get in there and become part of the action.

Smile, speak, listen.

CRITICISM

I do not resent criticism, even when, for the sake of emphasis, it parts for the time with reality.

WINSTON CHURCHILL
1874–1965

Constructive criticism can plant a seed
that, when nurtured, can bring about a
transformation in our chosen career or
hobbies. The fact that someone cares can
lift the spirit and fire the imagination.

**I am open to constructive criticism,
but closed to negativity.**

DEATH

Tell me, my soul, can this be death?

ALEXANDER POPE
1688–1744

The simple fact is that we cannot die. Our mind energy is attached to the physical body and brain until the body dies, then it leaves. But it doesn't disappear – it simply goes elsewhere. We judge ourselves, and choose a path to take us to the next step of our universal journey.

I cannot die. My mind is everlasting.

DETERMINATION

*Our deeds determine us, as much as we
determine our deeds.*

GEORGE ELIOT
1819–1880

Determination is a single-mindedness that produces results, but if it is taken to extremes it can isolate us. We all have to interact with one another to achieve lasting results. 'Moderation in all things' are wise words in this instance.

I will always balance determination with realisation.

DISCONTENT

And sigh that one thing only has been lent
To youth and age in common – discontent.

MATTHEW ARNOLD
1822–1888

If you are constantly discontented then you are under-achieving. Whenever you feel this way, you should decide whether it can be altered. If not, you should move on to something more exciting, more interesting. You have to make the effort – only you can make it work.

For heaven's sake, cheer up!

DISCRETION

A good man is merciful, and lendeth:
and will guide his words with discretion.
For he shall never be moved:
and the righteous
shall be had in everlasting remembrance.

PRAYER BOOK
1662

To be discreet is to care, not to want to hurt unduly. If you have a spontaneous personality, practise thinking before you speak, write or act. When you are angry, try to keep quiet until you have calmed down. One day it may save you from something nasty.

Discretion in all things.

EMBARRASSMENT

Jack was embarrassed – never hero more,
And as he knew not what to say, he swore.

LORD BYRON
1788–1824

The main cause of embarrassment is shyness, and it is a real problem. If this applies to you, then always choose your friends and partners carefully to avoid further unease. Shyness can be alleviated if you are able to laugh at yourself.

Laugh and the world laughs with you. Weep and you weep alone.

ENCOURAGEMENT

I wish you all the joy that you can wish.

WILLIAM SHAKESPEARE
1564–1616

If you are given encouragement from family, teachers and friends from an early age, then you are more likely to be successful in later life than those who received little or no encouragement at all. There are exceptions, but these people have to set out to prove themselves, come what may.

I will give encouragement wherever it is needed.

ENERGY

Energy is Eternal Delight.

WILLIAM BLAKE
1757–1827

We are energy beings first and foremost. But stress causes energy blockages in the physical body, causing distress and disease. Do not underestimate the power of the mind. Positivity counteracts negative energies, makes waves of love, compassion and understanding, and it heals.

Energy is life. Life is fantastic.

EXPECTATIONS

What we anticipate seldom occurs;
what we least expected generally happens.

BENJAMIN DISRAELI
1804–1881

Expectations are the main cause of unhappiness – expectancy of reward, perfect relationships, perfect children, perfect life. Forget it! The best you can hope for is to be treated with the same respect you give out. Accept your life as it is for the moment, and work towards your future dreams with light, love and laughter, for they are the jewels of life.

I will not have expectations of others. I will make it happen for myself.

FAITH

Faith consists in believing when it is beyond the power of reason to believe. It is not enough that a thing be possible for it to be believed.

VOLTAIRE
1694–1778

It is almost impossible if you have an analytical mind to have faith. Faith requires absolute belief in something which is beyond your control. Yet having faith in something good brings an added dimension to your life. Having faith in yourself is even better.

I will have faith in the good of others and belief in myself.

FAME

What is fame? an empty bubble;
Gold? a transient, shining trouble.

JAMES GRAINGER
c.1721–1766

The highs and lows of fame are legendary. Instead of seeking fame, why not simply enjoy your talent and your friends? If you are that good, fame will meet you half-way. So many deluded people waste their lives trying to exploit a talent that is moderate instead of living life to the full. Give yourself a chance to find the real you.

Fame is an empty vessel. Only I can decide what it will contain.

FATIGUE

Thinking is to me the greatest fatigue in the world.

SIR JOHN VANBRUGH
1664–1726

An excellent way of dealing with non-clinical fatigue is with meditation, or just day-dreaming. It takes the pressure of the mind energy off the brain and body, which removes energy blockages and results in rejuvenation of the whole system. Try it – give your mind and body a break!

Meditation every day keeps fatigue away.

FEAR

Let me assert my firm belief that the only thing we have to fear is fear itself.

PRESIDENT FRANKLIN

D. ROOSEVELT

1882–1945

Fear is destructive. It eats into our soul and disables constructive thought. If we face our fears and think them through to a positive end result, we will be taking control of our own lives, and this will strengthen our resolve to banish fear from our lives.

I must take positive action and face my fears.

FORGIVENESS

We read that we ought to forgive our enemies;
but we do not read that we ought to forgive our friends.

COSIMO DE' MEDICI
1389–1464

It is difficult to forgive, especially if the perpetrator of the crime appears to escape punishment. But if you hang on to all the anguish, you are the one who is going to feel it most. Get rid of your negative feelings and be an example to those around you. If you cannot forgive, then move on. There is always life after sorrow. Live and let live.

If I cannot forgive and forget, I must move on.

FUN

Fun is fun but no girl wants to laugh
all of the time.

ANITA LOOS
1893–1981

Fun is usually something you have when there is rapport within a group of people and there is a lot of leg-pulling and much laughter. We all need fun in abundance, so look for it wherever and whenever you can.

To release the tensions I am going to have fun.

GRIEVANCE

*Every time I make an appointment,
I make one ungrateful person and a
hundred with a grievance.*

LOUIS XIV
1638–1715

When grievances take over your mind, logical thought becomes impossible. All you want to hear is other people backing and strengthening your allegations. Holding a grievance, whether valid or not, is a great time waster and will affect your health. Next time you harbour a grievance, write it down, then destroy it.

Grievances can only lead to mental, physical and spiritual instability.

GUIDANCE

Shall then this verse to future age pretend
Thou wert my guide, philosopher, and
friend?

ALEXANDER POPE
1688–1744

From birth to the end of our lives we receive guidance from one source or another. The real test is separating the wheat from the chaff. The best way is to spend ten minutes a day evaluating the information: retain, separate and file. Sometimes what appears to be chaff turns out to be of real worth later.

Listen, use, save: the reward is logical, independent thought.

GUILT

There is nothing either good or bad,
but thinking makes it so.

WILLIAM SHAKESPEARE
1564–1616

If you are feeling guilty and are unable to forget your wrong-doing then you must find a way of putting things right. If you carry guilt around like a sack of coals it will destroy you. On the other hand, if someone is making you feel guilty and you feel that you are innocent, you must let them know what you are thinking so you can forget it.

I will deal with my own guilt and make others deal with theirs.

HATE

I hate and I love: why I do so you may well ask.
I do not know, but I feel it happen and am in agony.

CATULLUS
*c.*87–54 BC

To hate over a prolonged period will cause pain and suffering only to yourself. Hatred attracts negative energy that destroys everything in its path. Give yourself the third degree and ask whether it is worth all the misery. There are no winners in this game.

Hatred will consume my being. I must allow the light to return.

༄༅

JUDGEMENT

What judgement shall I dread, doing no wrong?

WILLIAM SHAKESPEARE
1564–1616

It is unwise to judge others, because the full facts are rarely available. Everyone's perception of the case differs according to their emotional involvement. Trying to get to the truth of the matter is like walking through a minefield, and you could be blown away. It is far better to listen than to judge.

Judge not – lest ye be judged.

KINDNESS

Tell them that, to ease them of their griefs,
Their fears of hostile strokes, their
aches, losses,
Their pangs of love, with other
incident throes
That nature's fragile vessel doth sustain
In life's uncertain voyage, I will some
kindness do them.

WILLIAM SHAKESPEARE
1564–1616

To be kind to others costs nothing, and yet in the course of a day so many unkind words and gestures are exchanged wherever there are groups of people together. We should think before we act or speak, then perhaps we can replace the intended action or words with a little kindness. It could completely change the atmosphere where you work, rest or play.

Kindness, like happiness, is catching.

KNOWLEDGE

Knowledge itself is power.

FRANCIS BACON
1561–1626

Knowledge comes in many guises: you can be totally ignorant one minute, enlightened the next. It also comes in small packages, enabling us to learn only what we need for the moment. We choose what we learn; we have freedom of choice over what we know.

Without knowledge there is no progress. Without progress I can only stand still.

LAUGHTER

I made hay while the sun shone.
My work sold.
Now, if the harvest is over
And the world cold,
Give me the bonus of laughter
As I lose hold.

SIR JOHN BETJEMAN
1906–1984

Laughter is the catalyst for all healing. It releases the tensions from mind and body, allowing the free flow of energy which, in turn, stimulates every organ throughout the system. This increases the circulation of blood and thus revitalises the cells.

Seeing the funny side of life keeps me happy and healthy.

LEISURE

*Increased means and decreased leisure
are the two civilizers of man.*

BENJAMIN DISRAELI
1804–1881

The faster the pace of life becomes, the more leisure time you need. Do not make excuses for not taking time off for leisure; the regrets you have later in life will be all the more poignant if you destroy yourself through lack of quality time.

Leisure is a pleasure I must not ignore.

LOVE

*She bore about with her, she could not help
knowing it, the torch of her beauty; she
carried it erect into any room that she
entered; and after all, veil it as she might,
and shrink from the monotony of bearing
that it imposed on her, her beauty was
apparent. She had been admired. She had
been loved.*

VIRGINIA WOOLF
1882–1941

When love touches a human soul, it changes it for ever. The eyes, which are the windows of the soul, take on a brilliance that is not of this world, for pure love comes from a source which we can only feel. If you have a special *unselfish* love for someone, then you can draw from this incredible energy.

To give love is to receive.

MATERIALISM

*The black and merciless things
that are behind the great possessions.*

HENRY JAMES
1843–1916

If you have a materialistic nature, you could miss out on so many beautiful experiences that cost nothing. The simple life could give you far more, in peace and harmony, than any material possessions. Check out how many things you could do without and save yourself a lot of hard work, heartache and money.

Inanimate objects cannot take the place of vibrant living things.

MEDITATION

Alas! I have nor hope nor health,
Nor peace within nor calm around,
Nor that content surpassing wealth
The sage in meditation found,
And walked with inward glory crowned.

PERCY BYSSHE SHELLEY
1792–1822

If you would like to try meditation in its simplest form, just sit down in a comfortable chair, close your eyes, and day-dream. Practise every day and you will soon be able to lose yourself in images that you have created with your mind. Creative imagination is the key to a less stressful life and a healthier lifestyle.

I will meditate every day to keep stress at bay.

MEMORIES

I've a grand memory for forgetting, David.

ROBERT LOUIS STEVENSON
1850–1894

Beautiful, happy memories enhance our lives, and we can learn from the bad ones. Our higher minds usually protect us from the extreme negative effects of the bad memories but strengthen the life-giving properties of the positive. For elderly people, happy memories are essential for health, so try to store a mass of memories for the future.

I will make a happy memory every day to ensure a bright future.

NOISE

How many a father I have seen
A sober man, among his boys,
Whose youth was full of foolish noise.

ALFRED, LORD TENNYSON
1809–1892

The world is so full of noise that we are becoming incapable of listening to our innermost thoughts, those messages that come from the part of the mind that touches the source of all inspiration. The noise factor has to be eliminated for at least an hour a day to maintain the health of our mind, body and spirit.

I need peace. I want my life back.

OPPORTUNITIES

*A wise man will make more opportunities
than he finds.*

FRANCIS BACON
1561–1626

If you have the opportunity to enhance your life, take it. If you don't, make sure you don't waste energy regretting a lost opportunity later. The majority of opportunities are lost through laziness, fear, or lack of self-confidence. Try to eradicate these obstacles from your life and you will be on a winning streak.

**I can rise above the fears.
I will not fail.**

PESSIMISM

The optimist proclaims that we live in the best of all possible worlds and the pessimist fears this is true.

JAMES BRANCH CABELL
1879–1958

Pessimism is the worst kind of negativity, because it does not allow any positive thoughts to intrude into the mind. The glass is always half empty, never half full. If you feel that you cannot be happy and have nothing to live for, then stir yourself and *make* something happen. Misery is the first thing that turns other people away.

My world must be full of colour.

POSITIVITY

Injustice, poverty, slavery, ignorance –
these may be cured by reform or revolution.
But men do not live only by fighting evils.
They live by positive goals, individual and
collective, a vast variety of them, seldom
predictable, at times incompatible.

SIR ISAIAH BERLIN
1909–1997

A positive outlook on life is your health insurance for the future. Where positivity is concerned, the thought is the deed. With practice, it will turn your life around, failure will be replaced with success, and your whole being will glow with health.

**Positive thought, success.
Negative thought, failure.**

POSSESSIVENESS

Being your slave, what should I do but tend
Upon the hours and times of your desire?
I have no precious time at all to spend,
Nor services to do, till you require.

WILLIAM SHAKESPEARE
1564–1616

Possessiveness is a misery for all concerned. Once drawn into this fatal web, it is very difficult to extract yourself from the deceiving but beautiful steel-like filaments that stifle all life from the victim. It also leads to a slow death for the perpetrators, because they cannot relax their vigil.

Possessiveness kills love.

PREDICTIONS

Mr Turnbull had predicted evil consequences . . . and was now doing the best in his power to bring about the verification of his own prophecies.

ANTHONY TROLLOPE
1815–1882

It is essential for everyone to build up
images of what they want to achieve,
and to hold that dream. This way you
are predicting your own future and your
life is in *your* hands. Predictions from
others take away that control and then
you become dependent.

**I will have complete control and
responsibility for myself.**

PRIDE

'The whole of this unfortunate business,'
said Dr Lyster, 'has been the result of
PRIDE AND PREJUDICE.'

FANNY BURNEY
1752–1840

Pride can prevent you asking for help when you need it most. I have known couples in desperate need who were too proud to ask their children for help, yet their offspring would have jumped at the chance of helping their parents. It is also true that pride goes before a fall, so if you need help, *ask for it.*

People need to be needed. I will ask for help when I cannot cope.

PRINCIPLES

I am afraid he has not been in the inside of
a church for many years;
but he never passes a church without
pulling off his hat.
This shews that he has good principles.

SAMUEL JOHNSON
1709–1784

Throughout life you will find that others will try to seduce you with promises of wealth. But in many cases, attaining it quickly or easily would mean that you have to forget your principles, and this would inevitably result in a downward trend in your life. It is much more important to build on the foundations of health and happiness.

Stick to your principles and you will have your just rewards.

PRIVACY

Private faces in public places
Are wiser and nicer
Than public faces in private places.

W. H. AUDEN
1907–1973

It is absolutely essential that everyone has some privacy in their lives. If you are desperate, there is always one small room in every house where no one can follow! With effort it can afford you a small amount of time to collect your thoughts. This room can be your salvation, especially if you have a crowded home.

Where there is a will, there is a way.

QUARRELS

*Thrice blest (and more) are the couple
whose ties are unbroken and whose love,
never strained by nasty quarrels, will not
slip until their dying day.*

HORACE
65–8 BC

However nice you are, it is extremely difficult to avoid quarrels. To protect our health we have to cut down the negative impact that quarrels have on us by ignoring stupid and unimportant issues. Save your energy for the important things in life, and especially for those who cannot fight for themselves.

I have time for intelligent conversation but I have no time for quarrels.

RETIREMENT

For solitude sometimes is best society,
And short retirement urges sweet return.

JOHN MILTON
1608–1674

Retirement can be either a very difficult time or the icing on the cake of life. To remain healthy, though, you should keep busy. There is something out there for everyone; you simply have to look for it. Retirement does not mean that you have to retire from life – it is the beginning of a New Life.

Life is for living.

SACRIFICES

The universe is so vast and so ageless that the life of one man can only be justified by the measure of his sacrifice.

PILOT OFFICER V. A. ROSEWARNE
1916–1940
Last letter to his mother, published in
The Times 18 June 1940

Parents continually make sacrifices for their children and, as the children grow up and the parents age, this is hopefully reciprocated. We need help at both ends of the age spectrum. If you are asked to make sacrifices to help someone, you will never regret it, because whatever you give you will eventually receive.

I am prepared to make sacrifices to help others.

SARCASM

Sarcasm is the lowest form of wit,
and the highest form of vulgarity.

ANON

If you have to resort to sarcasm, then you need to look at your whole personality structure. Young people are sarcastic when they feel threatened, but the sooner this phase is put behind them, the better. Such remarks are distasteful, hurtful, and can bring friendships to an end.

**If I can't say something nice,
I won't say anything at all.**

SCREAMING

His hilarity was like a scream from a crevasse.

GRAHAM GREENE
1904–1991

Screaming is good for you in small doses, but if it becomes a normal part of your everyday life then there is something very wrong. If things are getting you down, or you are grieving, have a short sharp scream to release the tension. Then stop and breathe deeply so that you will always be in control.

I might scream now and then, if it is really necessary.

SENSATIONALISM

The chapter on the Fall of the Rupee
you may omit.
It is somewhat too sensational.

OSCAR WILDE
1854–1900

There are many tragic things happening every day in our society which are sensationalised by the media. Children are being born into a world of high adrenaline attitudes and atmospheres. This is unhealthy and must change if we are to teach our children not to sensationalise every little thing that happens in their lives.

Truth and simplicity are the name of the game.

SIGN OF THE CROSS

Except ye see signs and wonders,
ye will not believe.

THE BIBLE, ST JOHN

The sign of the cross is a symbol of peace. If you have sleeping problems, make the sign of the cross on yourself, the door of your bedroom, and on your bed head or pillow. Whatever your religion, if you have insomnia or any other problems, do try it – you will find that it brings immediate peace.

With this sign I will have peace within.

SIMPLIFICATION

Our life is frittered away by detail . . .
Simplify, simplify.

HENRY DAVID THOREAU
1817–1862

Most people complicate their lives with so many small details that their minds are like rubbish tips. As you think, decide which thoughts are worthy of your attention and which should be thrown away. Then, when you can give your full attention to those you have retained, simplify. By doing this you can reduce the load.

Simplify. Simplify. Simplify.

SINCERITY

Sir, are you so grossly ignorant of human nature, as not to know that a man may be very sincere in good principles, without having good practice?

SAMUEL JOHNSON
1709–1784

Most people quickly recognise and avoid those who are insincere. If you cannot be sincere in your feelings when speaking to someone, then keep quiet or change the subject. Sincerity is absolutely essential if you wish to succeed. Nobody likes to be taken for a fool.

Sincerity is much the best option.

SINGING

My soul is an enchanted boat,
Which, like a sleeping swan, doth float
Upon the silver waves of thy sweet singing.

PERCY BYSSHE SHELLEY
1792–1822

Singing is the most wonderful exercise for the mind and body because it releases all the blockages throughout the system. It is exhilarating, and it doesn't matter one iota whether or not you have a good voice – it is how it makes you feel that is important. If others complain about your singing, sing when you are alone.

Singing exhilarates and rejuvenates.

SPIRITUALITY

*There is a spirituality about the face,
however . . . which the typewriter does not
generate. The lady is a musician.*

SIR ARTHUR CONAN DOYLE
1859–1930

Spirituality is how you activate the goodness in your mind for the benefit of mankind. Having the courage to combat the evils of this world adds to your spirituality. It is not an easy path to follow, but the love you will feel around you will be your reward.

My spirituality will be of my own making.

STABILITY

so much depends
upon
a red wheel
barrow
glazed with rain
water
beside the white
chickens.

WILLIAM CARLOS WILLIAMS
1883–1963

It is sometimes the little things in life which give us our stability. If children grow up in a stable home, they will cherish their memories for ever and, in turn, these memories will support them when they are most needed. No matter how many times you change your circumstances, always maintain some stability in your life.

I must be earthed so that I can fly.

STEALING

*To keep my hands from picking and
stealing, and my tongue from evil-speaking,
lying, and slandering.*

PRAYER BOOK
1662

Stealing is a crime against humanity. If you cannot obtain things through hard work and talent, then you have to go without. It is delightful to have nice things, but when they do not belong to you, how can you enjoy them? The spirit of the owner will always inhabit them and you will never know peace until they have been restored to their rightful owners.

I will never steal. The things I own must love me.

SUPERSTITION

There is a superstition in avoiding superstition.

FRANCIS BACON
1561–1626

If you are superstitious, then you will surely bring about that which you believe. Many superstitions sound ridiculous, but not to the people who have imprisoned themselves within the walls of these beliefs and turned them into a religion. Superstitions take away the freedom of thought, word and deed, because you believe you have no choice.

I always have a choice.

SURVIVAL

I survived.

ABBÉ EMMANUEL JOSEPH SIEYÈS
1748–1836

In life you simply cannot give up, no matter how bad things become. We all have our own in-built survival kit that will help us in desperate circumstances. Surviving has very little to do with courage but a lot to do with choice. When we have made the right choice and survived, the joy is indescribable, and we can be proud of our achievement.

I will survive.

Sympathy

It is the secret sympathy,
The silver link, the silent tie,
Which heart to heart, and mind to mind,
In body and soul can bind.

SIR WALTER SCOTT
1771–1832

We all need to feel the sympathy of our friends when we hit a bad patch in our lives. Knowing that we are not alone in times of stress can remove some of the impact of what we are experiencing, and aids recovery. Sympathy is not the same as feeling sorry for someone but is an emotion for which we are always truly grateful.

Sympathy is indescribable, and our lives are enhanced by it.

TEARS

With the persuasive language of tears.

CHARLES CHURCHILL
1731–1764

Tears are a safety valve for the emotional pressures that threaten to destroy our health. At some time during your sad periods, though, you must find the necessary discipline to stop. As in all things, there has to be balance.

Tears may flow, but there should be a limit.

TEASING

Speak roughly to your little boy,
and beat him when he sneezes;
He only does it to annoy
Because he knows it teases.

LEWIS CARROLL
1832–1898

Teasing can be the act of a friend to induce laughter. It can also be cruel. Cruel teasing is unwarranted and unnecessary, and shows a flaw in the character of the perpetrator. Kind teasing, however, is an excellent way of bringing laughter into someone's life, especially if they are feeling low.

Tease only when it brings happiness to others.

TEMPER

A tart temper never mellows with age, and a sharp tongue is the only edged tool that grows keener with constant use.

WASHINGTON IRVING
1783–1859

Getting into a temper might relieve stress, but it really does not achieve much. With such anger, words become meaningless, because all logical thought deteriorates. If you have a really bad temper, try to discover the root cause, because bad tempers can cause terrible problems which could ruin not only your life but also the lives of those around you.

I will not lose my temper. I will keep my self-respect.

TOLERANCE

The various modes of worship, which prevailed in the Roman world were all considered by the people as equally true; by the philosopher, as equally false; and by the magistrate, as equally useful. And thus toleration produced not only mutual indulgence, but even religious concord.

EDWARD GIBBON
1737–1794

Tolerance is a virtue that could be practised more often than it is. Try to look at the problems you have concerning others by reversing the situation. This process brings many things to light, and one of them might be your own intolerance. Think before you speak or act – it only takes a minute.

I will try to be more tolerant of others.

TOUCH

We must touch his weaknesses with a delicate hand. There are some faults so nearly allied to excellence that we can scarce weed out the fault without eradicating the virtue.

OLIVER GOLDSMITH
1730–1774

It is only by touching that we can pass on and receive healing energies that revitalise, renew, and touch our hearts, knowing that someone cares. Nothing can replace a loving touch on the arm when we are distressed, a finger stroking our face or, better still, a loving hug. These actions are priceless.

I will use touch to enhance the lives of others.

TRUTH

Dare to be true: nothing can need a lie;
A fault, which needs it most, grows two
thereby.

GEORGE HIBBERT
1593–1633

Truth does have a habit of winning the battle. For it *is* a battle – between the seemingly easy way out if you lie, or the harder way if you are honest. Tell the truth and get it over with, then you can relax. If you lie, stress will be your dubious playmate, and sooner or later you will be exposed for the liar that you are.

I speak the truth, and seek the truth.

VOCABULARY

Many terms which have now dropped out of favour will be revived, and those that are at present respectable will drop out, if usage so choose, with whom resides the decision and the judgement and the code of speech.

HORACE
65–8 BC

There is nothing quite so frustrating as trying to express yourself when you can't find the right phrase or word to do it. The dictionary is the greatest book in the world – every word is meaningful and expressive, and we should become acquainted with as many of them as possible. Words are magical, and it is never too late to bring more magic into your vocabulary.

My vocabulary can always be improved.

WALKING

*Who is the third who walks always beside
you?
When I count, there are only you and I
together
But when I look ahead up the white road
There is always another one walking beside
you.*

T. S. ELIOT
1888–1965

Walking is the one thing that, if fit, we can all do. Every day, without fail, we should walk until we are tired, then turn around and walk back, breathing deeper and feeling our lungs working overtime. Sounds exhausting? That's because you are out of practice, but don't worry – you have the rest of your life to catch up!

I am determined to walk a little further each day.

WORK

Perfect freedom is reserved for the man who lives by his own work, and in that work does what he wants to do.

R. G. COLLINGWOOD
1889–1943

Work keeps stress at bay. It is necessary to our health and happiness, and does not deserve the abuse that is often directed towards it. If you hate the work that you do but cannot change it for financial reasons, then find something that you love to do for a hobby – it could lead you down unexpected and lucrative paths.

Work is food for the soul.

WRITING

True ease in writing comes from art, not chance,
As thou move easiest who have learn'd to dance.
'Tis not enough no harshness gives offence,
The sound must seem an echo to the sense.

ALEXANDER POPE
1688–1744

There is nothing more satisfying than being able to put thoughts into words. Books are worlds within worlds, containing imagery and knowledge that can open up hitherto unknown avenues for the reader. The wonders of these worlds have been painstakingly written down, incorporating the talent and imagination of the writer. Writing is also therapeutic, and can cure many ills.

Without writing, ignorance would reign.

YOUTH

How beautiful is youth, that is always slipping away! Whoever wants to be happy, let him so: about tomorrow there's no knowing.

LORENZO DE' MEDICI
1449–1492

The elderly talk constantly about their youth, recalling incidents they know they cannot repeat. And yet the young are disdainful of their own few years. If you are young, do as many things as you can, and seek as much knowledge as you can, because in later life you will find great happiness recalling the memory of what you have been.

The mind, forever young, will overcome the ageing experience.

If you wish to receive distant healing, books, tapes or teaching brochures, please write to:

Betty Shine,
P.O.Box 1009,
Hassocks,
West Sussex,
BN6 8XS

Please enclose a stamped addressed envelope for a reply. Thank you.

About the author

Betty Shine is known worldwide for her powers as a medium and healer. She is the author of a number of bestselling books, including the *Sunday Times* No.1 bestseller *Mind Magic*. A former opera singer, Betty has been a medium, healer and hypnotherapist for over 20 years, and a vitamin and mineral therapist for 40 years.

'The world's number one healer'
The Sun